WISCONSIN

The Badger State

BY
JOHN HAMILTON

Abdo & Daughters

An imprint of Abdo Publishing | abdopublishing.com

abdopublishing.com

Published by ABDO Publishing, a division of ABDO, PO Box 398166, Minneapolis, Minnesota 55439. Copyright © 2017 by Abdo Consulting Group, Inc. International copyrights reserved in all countries. No part of this book may be reproduced in any form without written permission from the publisher. ABDO & Daughters™ is a trademark and logo of ABDO Publishing.

Printed in the United States of America, North Mankato, Minnesota.
082016
092016

Editor: Sue Hamilton   **Contributing Editor:** Bridget O'Brien
Graphic Design: Sue Hamilton
Cover Art Direction: Candice Keimig   **Cover Photo Selection:** Neil Klinepier
Cover Photo: iStock
Interior Images: Alamy, AP, Circus World Museum, Dreamstime, Edward Marek, Fort Crawford Museum, Getty, Granger, Green Bay Packers, Harley-Davidson Company, Hoshie, iStock, Jacobolus, John Hamilton, Johnsonville Sausage, Library of Congress, Marquette University, Mile High Maps, Milwaukee Brewers, Milwaukee Bucks, Mountain High Maps, One Mile Up, Paul Kane, Peshtigo Fire Museum, Port of Green Bay, Travel Wisconsin, U.S. Army Corps of Engineers, U.S. Postal Service, University of Wisconsin-Milwaukee, University of Wisconsin-Stout, View From Above, Wikimedia, Wisconsin Dells, & Wisconsin Historical Society.

Statistics: *State and City Populations*, U.S. Census Bureau, July 1, 2015 estimates; *Land and Water Area*, U.S. Census Bureau, 2010 Census, MAF/TIGER database; *State Temperature Extremes*, NOAA National Climatic Data Center; *Climatology and Average Annual Precipitation*, NOAA National Climatic Data Center, 1980-2015 statewide averages; *State Highest and Lowest Points*, NOAA National Geodetic Survey.

Websites: To learn more about the United States, visit booklinks.abdopublishing.com. These links are routinely monitored and updated to provide the most current information available.

Cataloging-in-Publication Data

Names: Hamilton, John, 1959- author.
Title: Wisconsin / by John Hamilton.
Description: Minneapolis, MN : Abdo Publishing, [2017] | Series: The United
     States of America | Includes index.
Identifiers: LCCN 2015957754 | ISBN 9781680783537 (lib. bdg.) |
     ISBN 9781680774573 (ebook)
Subjects: LCSH: Wisconsin--Juvenile literature.
Classification: DDC 977.5--dc23
LC record available at http://lccn.loc.gov/2015957754

CONTENTS

THE BADGER STATE

Wisconsin is a beautiful state filled with rolling hills, deep forests, miles of lakeshore, rustic red barns—and cheese. Wisconsin is often called America's Dairyland. It is the nation's number-one producer of cheese. The state's hard-working cows are also the source of huge quantities of sweet milk and butter.

There's more to Wisconsin than its dairy products. Many farms dot the countryside, but there are also bustling cities. Milwaukee, along the shores of Lake Michigan, has many thriving businesses and summer festivals. Farther north is Green Bay, home of the state's beloved Packers football team. Madison is Wisconsin's eco-friendly capital, and the home of world-class universities and health-care facilities.

In the early 1800s, prospectors came to Wisconsin to work in the state's lead mines. Many of them had no shelter during the winter, so they "lived like badgers" by digging dwellings into the sides of the hills. That is why today Wisconsin is nicknamed "The Badger State."

Wisconsin's Sand Island Light stands on the rocky shoreline of Lake Superior.

QUICK FACTS

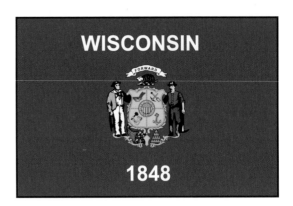

WISCONSIN

1848

Name: The name "Wisconsin" probably comes from an Ojibwe Native American word that describes the Wisconsin River.

State Capital: Madison, population 248,951

Date of Statehood: May 29, 1848 (30th state)

Population: 5,771,337 (20th-most populous state)

Area (Total Land and Water): 65,496 square miles (169,634 sq km), 23rd-largest state

Largest City: Milwaukee, population 600,155

Nickname: The Badger State; America's Dairyland

Motto: Forward

State Bird: Robin

State Flower: Wood Violet

State Rock: Red Granite

State Tree: Sugar Maple

State Song: "On, Wisconsin!"

Highest Point: Timms Hill, 1,951 feet (595 m)

Lowest Point: Lake Michigan, 579 feet (176 m)

Average July High Temperature: 81°F (27°C)

Record High Temperature: 114°F (46°C), in Wisconsin Dells on July 13, 1936

Average January Low Temperature: 6°F (-14°C)

Record Low Temperature: -55°F (-48°C), in Couderay on February 4, 1996

Average Annual Precipitation: 33 inches (84 cm)

Number of U.S. Senators: 2

Number of U.S. Representatives: 8

U.S. Postal Service Abbreviation: WI

QUICK FACTS

GEOGRAPHY

Wisconsin is in the Upper Midwest region of the United States. Its land and water area is 65,496 square miles (169,634 sq km). That makes it the 23rd-largest state. Bordering Wisconsin to the south is the state of Illinois. To the west are Iowa and Minnesota. To the north is Michigan. Wisconsin borders two of the Great Lakes. Lake Michigan is to the east, and Lake Superior is to the north.

Thousands of years ago, Ice Age glaciers slowly crept over Wisconsin. They scoured huge areas of land, creating flat plains and gently rolling hills. When the glaciers melted and retreated, they left behind clay, sediment, and silt—fertile soil for farming. Some of the glacier meltwater created the Great Lakes.

Ice Age glaciers created Wisconsin's flat plains and gently rolling hills.

Apostle Islands

LAKE SUPERIOR

MICHIGAN

Lac Vieux Desert

N

0   100 miles
0   100 km

Wisconsin River

WISCONSIN

Eau Claire

Mississippi River

Green Bay

MINNESOTA

Lake Winnebago

Green Lake

LAKE MICHIGAN

MICHIGAN

IOWA

Wisconsin River

Madison

Milwaukee

Kenosha

ILLINOIS

Wisconsin's total land and water area is 65,496 square miles (169,634 sq km). It is the 23rd-largest state. The state capital is Madison.

Wisconsin has five regions. Starting in the north, the Lake Superior Lowland is a narrow flatland that borders Lake Superior. There are sandy beaches as well as beautiful rocky shorelines. Just offshore are the Apostle Islands. They are a group of 21 small

Regions of Wisconsin

Lake Superior Lowland

Northern Highland

Central Plain

Western Upland

Eastern Ridges and Lowlands

islands that are part of the Apostle Islands National Lakeshore. Accessible only by boat, there are sea caves, beaches, and historic lighthouses to explore.

The Northern Highland region has igneous bedrock created by ancient volcanoes. It occupies much of the northern half of Wisconsin. Vast forests grow in this region. There are also thousands of lakes and streams. Wisconsin's highest point is in this region. It is Timms Hill, which rises 1,951 feet (595 m) above sea level.

The Central Plain is a crescent-shaped region south of the Northern Highland. It is in the middle of the state. The land is flatter, and rests atop sandstone bedrock. There is rich soil for farming.

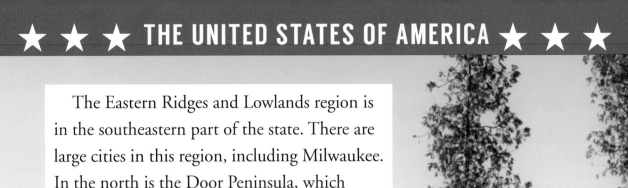

The Eastern Ridges and Lowlands region is in the southeastern part of the state. There are large cities in this region, including Milwaukee. In the north is the Door Peninsula, which sticks out of the eastern side of Wisconsin like a thumb. Popular with tourists, there are beautiful forests, orchards, and lakeshores.

The rugged Western Upland in the southwest is also called the Driftless Area. Glaciers did not affect this region. There are many ridges and valleys created by swift-flowing streams that cut into the limestone and sandstone bedrock. Forests mix with farmland in this region.

The Mississippi River forms much of Wisconsin's western border. The state's longest river is the Wisconsin River. It begins its journey in the northeast and winds its way 430 miles (692 km) through the state before emptying into the Mississippi River in the southwest.

Cave Point, Door Peninsula

CLIMATE AND WEATHER

Wisconsin has a humid continental climate, thanks to its location near the center of North America. Summers are usually hot and humid, while winters are long and cold. Temperatures are colder in the north, and warmer in the south. The growing season for crops is nearly six months in the south, but shrinks to about three months in the most northern parts of the state.

Besides normal summer thunderstorms, Wisconsin can be struck by extreme weather. The state is on the northern edge of Tornado Alley. On average, about 24 twisters whirl over Wisconsin each year.

A storm drops more than 1 foot (.3 m) of snow in Eau Claire, Wisconsin.

In winter, blizzards can dump 3 feet (.9 m) or more of snow. However, the weather is pleasant on most days in Wisconsin, especially during spring and autumn. In September and October, the leaves of the state's deciduous trees change to a stunning range of colors.

Statewide, Wisconsin's average July high temperature is 81°F (27°C). The state's hottest day occurred on July 13, 1936, in Wisconsin Dells. On that day, the thermometer soared to 114°F (46°C). In winter, the state's average January low temperature is 6°F (-14°C). On February 4, 1996, in the town of Couderay, the mercury plunged to a record low of -55°F (-48°C). Wisconsin receives an average of 33 inches (84 cm) of precipitation each year.

CLIMATE AND WEATHER

PLANTS AND
ANIMALS

Before European settlers arrived, 85 percent of Wisconsin was covered in forestland. Prairie grasses covered the rest. In the 1830s, settlers began clearing the land for farming. Lumberjacks chopped down countless acres of forests in the north. The landscape changed. Many animals lost their forest homes. Bison and caribou disappeared from the state.

Replanting has helped Wisconsin recover from over-logging. Today, about 49 percent of the state's land area is covered by forests. That is 17.1 million acres (6.9 million ha). Most of the forests are in the north and southwest. Tree species found in Wisconsin include aspen, birch, elm, maple, cottonwood, oak, white pine, jack pine, spruce, and fir. The official state tree of Wisconsin is the sugar maple. These sturdy hardwoods are famous for their brilliant yellow, orange, and red coloring in the autumn. Their sap is often collected in the early spring to make maple syrup.

A chipmunk nibbles a seed on a birch log.

Many kinds of wildflowers add splashes of color to Wisconsin's woodlands and prairies. They include wild blue phlox, dwarf lake iris, chicory, arrowhead, yellow flag iris, swamp milkweed, lupine, and columbine.

A fawn hides in a field of lupine and other wildflowers.

With all its different types of habitats, Wisconsin has a rich diversity of animal life. Black bears, coyotes, porcupines, beavers, snowshoe hares, and otters make their homes in the thick forests of the north. Gray wolves can sometimes be spotted—or heard howling—in the northern woods. Roaming over the entire state are white-tailed deer, rabbits, skunks, woodchucks, squirrels, and chipmunks.

Black Bear

Wisconsin's official state mammal is the badger. Short and stocky, with long, thick claws, these solitary animals spend most of the day in their underground dens. They can be bad-tempered fighters when disturbed.

Wisconsin is home to 55 native amphibian and reptile species. They include American toads, northern leopard frogs, spring peepers, spotted salamanders, eastern newts, snapping turtles, painted turtles, common garter snakes, and milk snakes. Two snake species are venomous: the eastern massasauga and the timber rattlesnake. They are found in the bluffs of southwestern Wisconsin. Like all snakes, these venomous reptiles are helpful to the state's ecosystems. They eat mice, voles, and rats. Although non-venomous snakes far outnumber venomous snakes in Wisconsin, hikers should take care when exploring. Look carefully before stepping over logs or climbing rocky ledges.

Garter Snake

Canada geese and a heron in the early morning mist of a Wisconsin lake.

Many kinds of birds make their homes in the forests, shorelines, and meadows of Wisconsin. They include gulls, orioles, sparrows, goldfinches, yellow-bellied sapsuckers, pileated woodpeckers, ruby-throated hummingbirds, anhingas, snowy egrets, herons, Canada geese, sandhill cranes, and pheasants. Wisconsin's state bird is the robin.

Lurking under the waves of Wisconsin's thousands of lakes and streams are 160 species of fish. They include largemouth and smallmouth bass, crappie, muskellunge, northern pike, yellow perch, walleye, bluegill, catfish, lake trout, rainbow trout, and Chinook salmon.

HISTORY

Long before European settlers arrived in Wisconsin, nomadic people came to the area to hunt large animals such as mammoths and bison. These Paleo-Indians were the ancient ancestors of today's Native

Paleo-Indians hunt a mammoth.

Americans. They traveled to the Wisconsin area about 12,000 years ago, after the last Ice Age glaciers melted.

As the centuries passed, several Native American cultures developed. By the time French explorers arrived in the 1600s, Wisconsin was settled by many tribes. They included the Ojibwe (also called the Chippewa), Sauk, Fox, Potawatomi, Menominee, Ho-Chunk (also called the Winnebago), and others.

An Ojibwe village by artist Paul Kane. The Ojibwe were also called the Chippewa.

French explorer Jean Nicolet landed on the Wisconsin shore in 1634.

The first European to visit Wisconsin may have been French explorer Étienne Brûlé. He explored the area around Lake Superior as early as 1622. However, the explorer who usually gets credit for being the first European on Wisconsin soil is Jean Nicolet. He arrived by canoe and came ashore near present-day Green Bay in 1634.

Wisconsin was a land rich with fur-bearing animals. Their pelts brought high prices in Europe. In the 1600s and 1700s, traders and trappers poured into the area. The French claimed control of Wisconsin during those early years. In 1763, Great Britain gained control of the area after winning the French and Indian War (1754-1763).

After the Revolutionary War (1775-1783), Great Britain gave up much of its North American territories, including Wisconsin, to the United States. Despite European and American claims to Wisconsin, people of the Sauk, Menominee, Ho-Chunk, Ojibwe, Fox, and Potawatomi tribes naturally wanted to control the land themselves, since they had been living there for hundreds of years.

As American fur trappers and settlers continued coming to Wisconsin, the Native Americans fought back. After several years of battles, they finally lost the struggle to keep their lands in 1832. That year, the United States Army battled Sauk Native Americans led by Chief Black Hawk. Hundreds of Native Americans were killed or captured during the Black Hawk War. Diseases such as smallpox also killed or weakened the native people. Most were forced to move to faraway reservations.

Fur trappers on a Wisconsin River.

The Martin Mine in Benton, Wisconsin, 1915.

The first metal ore mined in Wisconsin was lead. In the early 1800s, many immigrants arrived to work in the mines. By the middle of the "lead rush," about 4,000 miners dug 13 million pounds (5.9 million kg) of lead a year.

With resistance from the Native Americans broken, more settlers began pouring into the region. After lead was discovered in the southwest corner of Wisconsin, many immigrants rushed to the area to work in the lead mines. Lead was used to make pipes, paint, and ammunition. During the "lead rush," from the 1820s until the 1840s, Wisconsin produced half of all the lead used in the United States.

In 1836, the United States Congress created Wisconsin Territory. More and more settlers streamed in, attracted to the area's rich farmland and forests. In 1840, the population of Wisconsin was less than 31,000. Just 10 years later, the population swelled to more than 305,000. Many were immigrants from Ireland, Germany, and Norway.

On May 29, 1848, Wisconsin became the 30th state in the Union. Businessman and lawyer Nelson Dewey was the first governor of the state. The city of Madison became the state capital.

Governor Nelson Dewey

When the Civil War (1861-1865) broke out, Wisconsin fought on the side of the Union, and against slavery. The state sent about 91,000 men to fight in the war. More than 12,000 lost their lives.

After the war, settlers continued arriving in Wisconsin. Logging became an important industry to the state in the 1870s. Much of the dense, northern forestland was cut down by logging companies. (The forests would not recover until the 1900s.) In the 1880s, iron ore and copper mining boomed in northern Wisconsin. In the decades to come, millions of tons of iron ore were shipped by boat to cities in the East.

A logging crew near Marshfield, Wisconsin, around 1888. Much of Wisconsin's dense, northern forestland was cut down by logging companies.

During World War II, workers at Vilter Manufacturing and Chain Belt Company, both of Milwaukee, Wisconsin, produced products for the war effort, including guns and ammunition.

In 1929, the country's economy crashed with the start of the Great Depression. Many Wisconsinites lost their jobs, homes, and businesses. In addition, a severe drought gripped the Midwest in the early 1930s, which further hurt Wisconsin's farmers.

In the late 1930s, Wisconsin's economy began to improve. During World War II (1939-1945), several Wisconsin factories built products for the war effort. The state's farms produced needed dairy products for the nation. Today, the state continues to be a leading producer of cheese and milk.

In the late 20th century and early 2000s, Wisconsin diversified its economy. It continues to rely on agriculture and meatpacking, but the state is also home to many manufacturing businesses. Health care, education, and tourism have also become very important.

DID YOU KNOW?

• When Wisconsin was declared a territory of the United States in 1836, the Wisconsin government wanted to attract settlers to farm the land and start new towns. They bought newspaper advertisements and distributed brochures in Europe that declared how nice it was to live in Wisconsin. The state government even opened an office in New York City, New York, to coax people into moving west. The brochures and advertisements promised cheap land and a new start on the wild frontier. The brochures also heralded Wisconsin's "disease-free air." At that time, many people believed that diseases were caused by polluted air that hovered over big cities. For overpopulated areas like New York City or parts of Europe, the promise of disease-free air was a powerful reason to move to Wisconsin. The advertisements did their job: thousands of settlers streamed into Wisconsin. Most were from the New York City area, but many immigrants also came from Germany, Norway, Ireland, and other countries.

• In the late 1800s, reckless logging practices cleared entire forests. Waste wood, called "slash," was intentionally burned or left in piles. Extreme drought in 1871 made the landscape one big tinderbox. On the evening of October 8, 1871, strong winds whipped up small, smoldering slash fires in northeastern Wisconsin. The fires grew into a blaze that became the deadliest firestorm in American history. It burned more than 1.5 million acres (607,028 ha) of land and killed between 1,200 and 2,400 people (nobody knows the exact number). The inferno became known as the Peshtigo Fire, named after the Wisconsin town in which 800 people were burned to death. Not many people remember the Peshtigo Fire today because, on that same night, a much more famous fire occurred—the Great Chicago Fire of 1871.

DID YOU KNOW?

PEOPLE

Gene Wilder (1933-) is one of the most beloved Hollywood film actors of all time. He is also a screenwriter, producer, and novelist. Born and raised in Milwaukee, he first started acting in school plays. He received a theater arts degree from the University of Iowa. After serving in the United States Army, he began acting in stage plays in New York City, New York. From there, he went on to star in many Hollywood blockbusters, most of them comedies. His most popular films include *Willy Wonka and the Chocolate Factory* (1972), *Young Frankenstein* (1974), and *Silver Streak* (1976). Wilder shared an Academy Award nomination for Best Adapted Screenplay, along with director Mel Brooks, for *Young Frankenstein*.

Eric Heiden (1958-) is a long-track speed skating legend. In the 1980 Winter Olympic Games in Lake Placid, New York, he won five gold medals, setting four Olympic records and one world record. He is considered by many to be the best speed skater in history. Heiden was born in Madison, Wisconsin. He attended the University of Wisconsin-Madison, and eventually moved to California to become a medical doctor after his skating career. He was inducted into the United States Olympic Hall of Fame in 1983. In 1990, he was inducted into the Wisconsin Athletic Hall of Fame.

William Rehnquist (1924-2005) was the chief justice of the United States Supreme Court from 1986-2005. Born in Milwaukee, Wisconsin, he graduated first in his class from California's Stanford Law School in 1952. He worked in Washington, DC, as a law clerk to Supreme Court Justice Robert Jackson. Then, after working as a lawyer in his own law practice for many years, he worked in the Justice Department as an assistant attorney general. He was appointed in 1971 to the Supreme Court by President Richard Nixon. He was appointed chief justice in 1986 by President Ronald Reagan. Rehnquist was a conservative justice who believed in a strict following of the United States Constitution.

Harry Houdini (1874-1926) was a world-famous magician and escape artist. He was born in Hungary, but his family moved to Appleton, Wisconsin, when he was young. He often told people that Appleton was his hometown. Houdini began his career as a trapeze artist and magician, but he became famous as a person who could escape handcuffs and straightjackets. A popular showman, he thrilled audiences by being shackled with chains, placed in a locked crate, dropped into water, and then quickly escaping. He could also escape from a straightjacket while dangling upside down from a tall building. Later in life, Houdini made it his mission to expose frauds who claimed they could talk to dead people, and other spiritualists. Houdini died on Halloween, October 31, 1926, probably from an infected appendix.

CITIES

Madison is the capital of Wisconsin. It is the state's second-largest city, with a population of about 248,951. It is in the south-central part of the state. Native American tribes of Sauk, Fox, and Ho-Chunk people were early inhabitants of the area. The city was chosen as the state capital in 1836. It was named after President James Madison. Today, Madison is a center for high-tech industry, health care, and education.

Capitol Rotunda

One of the city's largest employers is the University of Wisconsin-Madison. It enrolls more than 43,000 students. Madison is filled with bike paths, parks, museums, theaters, and farmer's markets. Beautiful Lake Mendota is a popular spot for water sports such as boating, fishing, and swimming.

Milwaukee is the largest city in Wisconsin. Its population is about 600,155. It is located in southeastern Wisconsin, along the shores of Lake Michigan. It began as a fur-trading center in the late 1700s. The name Milwaukee is probably a Potawatomi or Ojibwe Native American word for "gathering place by the water." Milwaukee's importance grew in the 1800s as a shipping center and a national railroad hub. Breweries and manufacturing plants created a lot of jobs. Today, there are many kinds of businesses in the city. Manufacturing is still strong, but health care, insurance, and financial services are also important. Milwaukee is often nicknamed the "City of Festivals." In addition to the Wisconsin State Fair, the city hosts Summerfest, one of the largest music festivals in the world. The city is also famous for its museums. The Milwaukee Art Museum contains nearly 25,000 works of fine art.

Green Bay is Wisconsin's third-largest city. Its population is about 105,207. It is located in the northeastern part of the state. It rests along the shores of the Bay of Green Bay, a part of Lake Michigan. Green Bay is the oldest city in Wisconsin. It was first settled by French fur traders in the 1600s. It was named Green Bay because of the green tint of the water in the springtime. The city grew in the 1800s as a center for the logging industry. Today, Green Bay has many kinds of businesses. The biggest employers are paper mills, meatpacking plants, and health care. Tourism and agriculture are also big. The city is famous for being the home of the Green Bay Packers football team, which was founded in 1919. Green Bay is the smallest city to host a National Football League team.

Kenosha is in the southeastern corner of Wisconsin, along the shores of Lake Michigan. Its population is about 99,858. Once a manufacturing center, the city today is also home to industries such as education, health care, and tourism. The city's Dinosaur Discovery Museum includes the fossilized bones of many prehistoric beasts, including a *Tyrannosaurus rex*.

Eau Claire is located in west-central Wisconsin. Its population is approximately 67,778. Its name is a French phrase that means "clear waters." Logging and paper mills were big businesses in the late 1800s. Today, health care and education are major employers. The University of Wisconsin-Eau Claire enrolls more than 11,000 students. It is a top university for forestry and environmental research.

TRANSPORTATION

Port of
Green Bay

Wisconsin's first European explorers and fur trappers used the Great
Lakes to move about and transport their goods. As fur trading
increased, the traders began using the area's many rivers. Later,
canals and harbors were built for larger ships.

Railroads were built across the state in the mid-1800s. Railroads helped
farmers transport their crops quickly and easily to distant cities. Today,
there are 8 freight railroads operating in Wisconsin. They haul cargo on
3,449 miles (5,551 km) of track. The most common goods hauled by
rail are sand and gravel, farm products, coal, minerals, lumber and paper
products, and chemicals. Amtrak's Empire Builder line whisks passengers
across the state, from the Illinois border in the south to Milwaukee,
Madison, and on to the Minnesota border in the west. The Hiawatha line
provides regular service between Milwaukee and Chicago, Illinois.

Almost one-fourth of freight tonnage shipped on the Great Lakes is loaded from Wisconsin ports. Large cargo ships regularly drop anchor in Green Bay and Superior, Wisconsin.

Wisconsin has eight large commercial airports. The busiest is Milwaukee's General Mitchell International Airport. It serves about 6.5 million passengers yearly.

Wisconsin has 115,145 miles (185,308 km) of public roadways. Most major cities are served by interstate highways.

Wisconsin has several Scenic Byways. These roads take travelers through some of Wisconsin's most beautiful areas.

NATURAL
RESOURCES

Wisconsin's climate and rich soil make it a good place for farming. There are about 68,900 farms in the state. They occupy approximately 42 percent of Wisconsin's land area. The majority of the farms are small and family owned.

The most valuable agricultural product is dairy. Wisconsin is the top producer of cheese in the country. It ranks second in milk production (behind California). Important crops grown in the state include corn, soybeans, hay, potatoes, cranberries, wheat, apples, peas, onions, cherries, and barley. Besides dairy cows, Wisconsin's top livestock products are broiler chickens, turkeys, and hogs.

A manufacturer ages 4,000 wheels of cheese in a storeroom in Thorp, Wisconsin.

A cranberry harvest in Wisconsin.

Wisconsin's many marshes and sandy bogs make it a great place for growing cranberries. At harvest time, the marshes are flooded. The tart, red berries have small pockets of air inside them, so they float to the surface. That makes them easier to harvest. Wisconsin is the top cranberry grower in the United States. It produces more than 60 percent of the nation's total harvest.

About 49 percent of Wisconsin's land area is covered by forests. The state's logging industry produces paper, pulp, and furniture products.

In the past, lead and iron ore were Wisconsin's most valuable mineral products. Today, most of the state's mines and quarries produce limestone, crushed stone, plus sand and gravel.

NATURAL RESOURCES

INDUSTRY

Manufacturing provides many jobs in Wisconsin. Milwaukee and the surrounding area is a major center for machinery production. Kohler is a leading Milwaukee maker of small engines for industrial equipment, and is one of the state's leading employers. Wisconsin is also a top producer of metal products, computer equipment, paper, and food products.

There are many well-known companies that are based in Wisconsin, or have major operations in the state. The Harley-Davidson Company, the motorcycle manufacturer, has it headquarters in Milwaukee. Other famous companies in the state include Johnsonville Sausage, S.C. Johnson & Son, GE Healthcare, and Trek Bicycle.

The Harley-Davidson Company was founded in 1903 in Milwaukee. The motorcycle company is known for its line of big, powerful cruisers.

Johnsonville Sausage headquarters is located in Sheboygan Falls, Wisconsin. Founded in 1945, it has grown to be one of the largest sausage manufacturers in the country.

About 25 percent of the state's workforce is in the service industry. Instead of making products, service industry companies sell services to other businesses and consumers. It includes businesses such as banking, financial services, health care, restaurants, and tourism. Major insurance companies are located in Madison and Wausau.

Tourism is a huge industry in Wisconsin. Hunting, fishing, and camping are very popular pastimes. Wisconsin's dense forests are home to many kinds of wildlife. The state has more than 15,000 lakes, and about 84,000 miles (135,185 km) of rivers and streams. That is enough to circle the Earth three times.

More than 105 million visitors spend about $19 billion in the state yearly. That supports more than 190,000 jobs.

INDUSTRY

SPORTS

It is hard to get very far in Wisconsin without hearing about the Green Bay Packers. They are a professional National Football League (NFL) team based in the city of Green Bay. They are the last of the small-town teams, which were common in the 1920s. Earl "Curly" Lambeau helped form the team in 1919, and became their first coach. The team currently plays at Green Bay's Lambeau Field, which is named after its founder. The Packers have won four Super Bowls. The have also won more league championships than any other team.

Besides the Packers, Wisconsin is home to two other professional major league sports teams. The Milwaukee Brewers are a Major League Baseball (MLB) team. The Milwaukee Bucks play in the National Basketball Association (NBA). They won the NBA Finals championship in 1971.

Bucky Badger is the mascot for the University of Wisconsin-Madison.

The Golden Eagle is the mascot for Marquette University.

Pounce Panther is the mascot for the University of Wisconsin-Milwaukee.

The Wisconsin Badgers, of the University of Wisconsin-Madison, include men's and women's teams in sports such as hockey, football, basketball, and many others. Other popular college teams include the University of Wisconsin-Milwaukee Panthers and the Marquette Golden Eagles.

Outdoor lovers have many sports to choose from in Wisconsin. There are thousands of miles of hiking and biking trails in the state. Boating is very popular. In winter, many people enjoy skiing, snowmobiling, ice fishing, and even dogsledding.

SPORTS

ENTERTAINMENT

There are dozens of yearly festivals held in Wisconsin. Oktoberfest celebrates the state's many German immigrants and their descendants. It is held in many cities throughout the state in the autumn. Milwaukee's Festa Italiana is the largest Italian-American festival in America. The Swiss celebrate the William Tell Festival in New Glarus. Indian Summer Festival promotes Native American culture in Milwaukee. Norwegians flock to the Syttende Mai celebration in Stoughton.

There are museums of every type in Wisconsin, from small county exhibits to nationally known galleries of art and history. The Circus World Museum is in Baraboo, hometown of the Ringling brothers. It has a huge collection of circus wagons, posters, and other objects highlighting the history of the Ringling Brothers and Barnum & Bailey Circus.

Milwaukee's Harley-Davidson Museum has exhibits spanning more than 100 years, including more than 450 historic Harley-Davidson motorcycles and behind-the-scenes tours. The Experimental Aircraft Association AirVenture Museum is in Oshkosh. It preserves more than 200 historic airplanes.

Wisconsin Dells is one of the most-visited tourist sites in the state. The town is home to many thrill rides, water parks, and campgrounds. Nearby is the Dells of the Wisconsin River, a 5-mile (8-km) section of river with a gorge, tall cliffs, and spectacular sandstone formations.

Wisconsin Dells is known as the "Water Park Capital of the World."

ENTERTAINMENT

TIMELINE

10,000 BC—Paleo-Indians arrive in present-day Wisconsin.

1600—Native Americans established in the Wisconsin area include the Ojibwe, Sauk, Fox, Potawatomi, Menominee, and Ho-Chunk tribes.

1634—Jean Nicolet explores parts of Wisconsin.

1673—French explorers Father Jacques Marquette and Louis Joliet travel from Lake Michigan to the Mississippi River.

1763—Great Britain gains control of Wisconsin after winning the French and Indian War.

1764—Charles Langlade moves to Green Bay. He founds the first permanent settlement in Wisconsin.

1783—Great Britain loses control of Wisconsin to the United States after the American Revolution.

1832—Many Native Americans are killed or forced to leave their land in the aftermath of the Black Hawk War.

1836—Wisconsin Territory formed.

1848—Wisconsin becomes the 30th state in the Union.

1857—Railroad completed from Milwaukee to Prairie du Chien.

1861-1865—About 91,000 Wisconsin soldiers serve during the Civil War. More than 12,000 lose their lives.

1941-1945—More than 332,000 Wisconsin residents serve in the United States military during World War II. More than 8,000 die during the war.

1980—Eric Heiden of Madison wins five gold medals in speed skating at the Winter Olympic Games in Lake Placid, New York.

2011—The Green Bay Packers win their fourth Super Bowl championship.

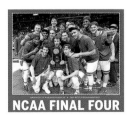

2015—The University of Wisconsin-Madison Badgers men's basketball team makes it to the Final Four of the NCAA Men's Division I Basketball Tournament.

TIMELINE

GLOSSARY

BLACK HAWK WAR

A series of battles in 1832 between white settlers and Sauk Native Americans under the leadership of Black Hawk.

DECIDUOUS

A tree or other plant that sheds its leaves each autumn.

ECOSYSTEM

A biological community of animals, plants, and bacteria that live together in the same physical or chemical environment.

GLACIER

Huge, slow-moving sheets of ice that grow and shrink as the climate changes. During the Ice Age, some glaciers covered entire regions and measured more than one mile (1.6 km) thick. Glaciers once covered much of present-day Wisconsin.

GREAT DEPRESSION

A time of worldwide economic hardship beginning in 1929. Many people lost their jobs and had little money. The Great Depression finally eased in the mid-1930s, but didn't end until many countries entered World War II, around 1939.

ICE AGE

A geological period of cold climate, with thick sheets of ice and snow covering the polar regions and expanding over the continents. The last major Ice Age peaked approximately 20,000 years ago.

IGNEOUS ROCK

Rock formed by the cooling of molten magma.

Immigrant

A person settling in a new country, after leaving their former homeland.

Lake Michigan

One of the Great Lakes. The state of Michigan is on Lake Michigan's eastern shore. Wisconsin is on its western shore.

Lake Superior

The largest of the Great Lakes. Lake Superior borders Michigan, Wisconsin, Minnesota, and Canada.

Sedimentary Rock

Rock that is formed by a slow process, over millions of years, of pressing together small particles such as sand and silt.

Tornado Alley

An area of the United States that has many tornadoes each year. There is no official boundary for Tornado Alley. Many maps show that it stretches from Texas in the south to North Dakota in the north. Some sources say it reaches east all the way to western Ohio.

University of Wisconsin

A statewide system of public universities. It was created by the Wisconsin legislature in 1848, and began the first class in Madison with 17 students in 1849. Officially called the University of Wisconsin System, it currently has 13 university campuses in cities all over the state, and enrolls more than 182,000 students.

World War II

A conflict that was fought from 1939 to 1945, involving countries around the world. The United States entered the war after Japan bombed the American naval base at Pearl Harbor, in Oahu, Hawaii, on December 7, 1941.

INDEX